forever flowers

Margaret Ashbourne

forever flowers

THE NEW APPROACH TO DECORATING WITH FAKE FLOWERS

photography by Sian Irvine

jacqui
small

*To George, Cameron, Alicia
and Sebastian*

First published in 2009 by
Jacqui Small LLP
7 Greenland Street
London NW1 0ND

Text copyright
© Margaret Ashbourne 2009
Photography, design and
layout copyright
© Jacqui Small 2009

Publisher Jacqui Small
Editorial Manager Lesley Felce
Designer Maggie Town
Editor Sian Parkhouse
Production Peter Colley

Additional photography by Craig Fordham
on pages 10, 16, 38, 40, 41 (below),
49 (above), 57 (below left and right),
92 (above left), 110, 117

ISBN 978 1 906417 22 2

A catalogue record for this book is available
from the British Library.

2011 2010 2009

10 9 8 7 6 5 4 3 2 1

Printed in Singapore

contents

Introduction 6

DESIGNING WITH FAKE FLOWERS 8
Simple Arrangements 10
More Complex Designs 18
Using Containers 26
Repeat Designs 34
Use of Colour 38
Planted Designs 46
Greenery and Grasses 52
Four Ways with Roses 56
Four Ways with Orchids 58

SPRING FLOWERS 60
Spring Flower Gallery 62
Spring Flowers in the Home 66
Spring Wedding 74
Easter Breakfast 78

SUMMER FLOWERS 82
Summer Flower Gallery 84
Summer Flowers in the Home 88
Summer Wedding 96
Al Fresco Lunch 100

AUTUMN FLOWERS 104
Autumn Flower Gallery 106
Autumn Flowers in the Home 110
Harvest Supper 118
Halloween Buffet 122

WINTER FLOWERS 126
Winter Flower Gallery 128
Winter Flowers in the Home 132
Christmas 140
Valentine Supper 144

WORKING WITH FAKE FLOWERS 148
Setting Flowers in Resin 150
Arranging without Water 152
Ringing the Changes 155
Maximizing Single Stems 156
Hand-tied Arrangements 157

Directory of Suppliers 158
Author's Acknowledgements 160

introduction

OPPOSITE This stone urn full of summer flowers was the centrepiece for our stand at the Chelsea Flower Show in London. It contains many flowers grown in English gardens and is based on a Dutch flower painting from the sixteenth century. This arrangement was made several years ago, but I love it so and to me it epitomizes the beauty of all flowers, whether real or hand-painted fakes.

BELOW A hand-painted old English rose.

The 'still life' arrangement opposite demonstrates the beauty of artificial flowers: they can add as much ambience to a room as a glorious painting. I feel that they are almost like three-dimensional paintings; they play an integral part in making our homes bright, cheerful and full of life, when overcrowded schedules do not allow time to gather fallen petals and replace the brackish water that fresh flowers produce.

We travel extensively for our flower business and the production of each flower never ceases to amaze me. Each petal, leaf and stem is individually cut out and hand painted, before being assembled, again by hand, to make each bloom perfect. One day, I was asked to paint the petals for a rose – but after two hours I had to admit defeat. I then found out it takes up to three years to train the flower painters, so it is hardly surprising that I failed so abysmally. On another occasion I watched a sample of a lupin being produced. Many days had already been spent making the stem, leaves and flowers, leaving just the tiny buds at the top to be made. It took

several more days of intricate work just to make those tiny buds!

The material used in the production of the flowers varies enormously but is rarely silk, although this word is synonymous with all artificial flowers. More important even than the type of materials used is the coating that is added afterwards. A few years ago, 'real touch' was developed. This was an exciting transition, making it even more difficult to tell the difference between real and fake flowers. We now add scent to some of our flowers, so three senses are accommodated – sight, touch and smell.

We live in a house called Ruckley in the English countryside – Ruckley also being the name of our flower company. Many years ago I became interested in dried flowers simply because I had so little time available to constantly replenish fresh flowers in my house. After my first harvest, a financial disaster, my husband insisted I repeat the process in order to repay the loan he had made me; this meant I had to be a lot more professional. I treasure the photographs I have of fields of flowers all in full bloom. Several years later, we ended up growing in several other countries and sourced seed heads throughout the world. (I still have not managed to pay back my husband!) Silk flowers came later as the fashion for dried flowers diminished and the quality of faux flowers improved. Throughout this book you will see our beautiful arrangements using artificial flowers, with the occasional inclusion of dried seed heads.

We have shown how these arrangements work equally well in both modern and traditional settings, so there will be something to appeal whatever your taste, age or lifestyle. The final chapter will help you if you wish to make your own designs; but whether you choose to do this or to buy a ready-made arrangement, I hope to have inspired you and passed on my passion for all flowers, both real and artificial.

designing with fake flowers

This section illustrates the use of seasonal flowers to make simple, natural-looking arrangements. We have used only one or two varieties in each vase, rather than mixing half a dozen or so flower types. They are made using flowers found in most gardens, and are designed to resemble posies that you might have picked yourself.

simple arrangements

My passion for all flowers began at the early age of three, which is as far back as I remember. One spring evening, while living in Hungerford, I went out with a young friend and her mother and we picked violets and primroses from the hedgerows. Today this would be frowned upon, but that evening remains a treasured and unforgettable memory for me.

Pansies are the next flowers that I remember well, as I once picked all my mother's treasured blooms from her garden and was not very popular after this. I, however, was delighted with the velvety petals, the brilliant colours and their smiling faces. When I was about five years old a very ancient aunt (knowing my delight in flowers) sent me through the post an old tin box full of primroses with their stems held in damp cotton wool. Received at such a young age, this was a never-to-be-forgotten present.

The picture opposite shows bluebells and muscari, or grape hyacinths, very naturally arranged in a glass vase. At Ruckley we have wonderful natural woodlands that are carpeted with these wonderful flowers, growing wild, and giving out the most delicious perfume. These are, of course, the natural English bluebells, rather than the hybridized *Hispanica* variety.

Another of my favourite flowers from childhood are the spring crocuses shown on this page. The meaning for crocus is cheerfulness – and they are such harbingers of spring. Certainly for me this simple group, 'growing' out of their bulbs and placed into pale blue glasses, gives as much pleasure as seeing their real counterparts appearing in the garden year after year.

LEFT These flower heads of white lilac and lime green *Viburnum opulus* share a light and airy beauty that makes for a perfect partnership. These are set in acrylic water to balance the weight of the flowers, but this is not always necessary.

OPPOSITE A collection of six linked tall glass bud vases, each containing a different spring flower or leaf.

Some of my favourite simple designs are based on displaying single stems, and faux flowers and foliage lend themselves very well to this approach. Green and white is a wonderful combination, and to me they are the epitome of spring freshness. I love to put together individual stems of leaves and flowers that represent the burgeoning countryside at that time of year.

On the page opposite we show a simple linked design. From left to right, the first bud vase contains pure white snowdrops, the first flower to appear at the end of January, often pushing their heads through icy ground. We grow many varieties at Ruckley but this *Galanthus nivalis* is the most popular type. Next, spring green ferns, as if just picked from the woods; then pure white magnolia, which is another early harbinger of spring; after this comes the later flowering cow parsley, which in late spring adorns all English hedgerows and country lanes; and fifth trailing yellow catkins as picked from the hazelnut tree. Lastly, immature oak leaves showing tiny baby acorns. This selection of vases can be grouped randomly but together they give far more impact and form a wonderful montage of the joy spring flowers and foliage can offer, across the whole of the season.

Our mail order catalogue is called 'Peony' as these are such wonderful flowers – the arrangement opposite is simple and informal. We use so many different types of peonies in our work, both hybrid peonies and also the far more unusual Chinese tree peonies. You will find them featured in many of our arrangements and I grow many varieties in my garden at Ruckley. Real peonies live for such a short time and their season is over far too quickly, so these artificial flowers allow us to enjoy them for a much longer time.

The display below contains freesias and white gerberas with green centres. This green centre is echoed in the green heads of *Viburnum opulus,* giving a wonderfully fresh feel to this arrangement. I chose to place this harmonious selection in a blue-and-white porcelain bowl to echo the backdrop of hand-painted Chinese silk wallpaper, but it would fit equally well in a modern container and setting.

OPPOSITE White peonies, just opening, the flower heads nestled among their bright green leaves, are gathered into a naïve handmade two-handled terracotta container.

RIGHT Heads of white gerberas, white freesias and lime green *Viburnum opulus*, or snowball plant, displayed in a blue-and-white hand-painted porcelain bowl. A piece of dry floral foam or some scrunched up chicken wire hidden in the bottom of the bowl helps to hold the short stems in position.

ABOVE A footed glass bowl of sweetpeas in cream, pink, and mauve shows their delicate airy form. Arrange these exactly as you would fresh sweetpeas, adding individual stems and trimming their length as necessary until you have a pleasing overall shape.

OPPOSITE This beautiful ruby glass vase is the perfect shape for this white camellia: its flared open top supports the large flower head and foliage and balances their weight.

Sweetpeas are one of the most popular of all our faux flowers – everyone's favourite. Very few English gardens would be complete without these deliciously scented summer flowers. The ones we have featured here are the annual variety rather than the longer stemmed perennial type, which are normally deep pink or white. We carry the full spectrum of colours of annual sweetpeas from white through pink, blue, violet and deep burgundy. Everyone has their own favourite, although most people choose a mixed bunch of all colours to create as natural-looking an arrangement as possible. The matching perfume spray makes them indistinguishable from those you would pick in your own garden – except, of course, that their beauty will endure for much longer.

What could be more appealing in January and February than the sudden blooming of these magnificent camellias, shown opposite? With their brilliant white flowers against dark, glossy leaves they are shown to perfection. The tiny buds complete the picture for a completely natural effect. In our garden we also grow bright pink and red coloured camellias, so of course we also carry both these colours as faux flowers. The tragic problem of the wonderful living plants is that a slight touch of frost or rain renders all the flowers brown and soggy, so having the faux copies is a wonderful bonus.

This section features designs that are slightly larger in scale and many contain combinations of several varieties of flowers. We start with spring varieties and finish with exotic material and orchids; the colours range from purest white to the brightest orange. Some designs are more suited to a traditional home and others follow simpler lines for a modern house.

OPPOSITE This linear display of white tulips and twigs is set in a narrow glass vase. Push the twigs in first, cut to a uniform height, and then push the multi-headed tulip stems through them, so that they act as support.

BELOW Combine different varieties of one flower, such as these mixed tulips, for a colourful display. The unusual twig basket can be made by sticking varied lengths of natural woody stems to double-sided tape wrapped around a plastic pot.

more complex designs

Because of my love of flowers, I use real and fake ones most days. I do find it slightly annoying, however, when the fresh ones will not bend in the way that I want them to; nor does the most open flower, on say a long stem of garden roses, appear in the position I want it too. Particularly annoying too, are flowers such as blossom which seem to shed petals almost as fast as I put them in water. Nonetheless one single enormous, beautifully scented flower from the *Magnolia grandiflora* growing outside my French window most certainly compensates for all the small annoyances of fresh flowers. Therefore in my living room at home I will have perhaps one single lovely fresh bloom, or small bunch of fresh flowers, living happily alongside three or four arrangements such as those shown on these pages.

In the narrow glass vase opposite the stark rigidity of the bare twigs is softened by the beauty and movement of the large white tulips and leaves and would look stunning against a plain wall. I have used faux wooden twigs, but if you make this arrangement yourself, then there are several varieties of winter twigs that can be used to equal effect.

On the left is a rustic twig basket from which bursts a shower of brilliant and impressive tulips, the colours of which are vivid and would certainly give a sharp impact to a dark corner. We have used several different varieties as well as different colours, including pointed modern tulips, as well as ancient parrot and the more readily available rounded species.

Fake flowers lend themselves quite happily to the contemporary style of sculptural arrangements because they are much easier to manipulate than fresh ones. You can afford to be quite brutal to achieve the effect you want! A good example of this is the arrangement of roses and leaves opposite. This is a rather difficult arrangement to make, though the finished result is worth the effort involved. Each individual rose leaf is loosely rolled and then glued to its neighbour. The whole vase has been filled with these leaves from which burst a lovely hand-tied bunch of rose buds in varying stages of opening. The roses themselves are beautifully shaded from creamy white to deep pink. Keeping the roses as a separate tied bunch means that the leaves and vase can be re-used over and over, with different flowers. A hand-tied bunch of sunflowers or dahlias would look delightful in autumn, or some multi-coloured ranunculus or peonies in the summer.

Lining glass bowls with twining stems serves two purposes: it adds another level of interest to a display, and the stems themselves can act as support for short-stemmed individual flower heads. The round bowl shown below looks good when viewed from above, and equally decorative when viewed from the sides.

OPPOSITE Rolled rose leaves line the glass vase and hide the twiggy stems of this hand-tied bouquet of pink roses. Using flowers at various stages of opening gives a far more natural look.

RIGHT Lengths of flowering honeysuckle are wrapped round and round inside the glass bowl, and interspersed with freesias and roses. A spray of perfume would be the perfect addition.

I love cutting long stems of flowering branches from trees and shrubs in my garden to bring into the house, but it can be tricky sometimes to find enough stems of uniform length to create a really good display. Also I don't want to leave my garden looking too de-nuded just when plants are at their peak. Faux flowering stems make excellent alternatives. The arrangement opposite is a stunning display of double white lilac and sharp green *Viburnum opulus*. I placed a few extra stems of both these flowers in the vase to give added impact. The vase itself echoes the colouring as it is a wonderful limey green shade and the light from the window adds another dimension. The colouring of the lilac itself is particularly lovely – the shading from white to palest green is both pleasing and authentic. A stem of lilac is perhaps one of the most difficult fake flowers to make. Each tiny flower has to be cut out and assembled. Most of the flowers are slightly different from each other in both size and colour, as are all the minute green buds. If you look at real lilac, the colour differs from stem to stem, showing the growth of the tree from year to year, and also the pruning that took place following the removal of the dead flowers from the previous year. All of this botanical detail is faithfully replicated in the lilac shown here.

Traditional floristry techniques, such as layering, transfer easily to fake flower displays. Different flowers have been used to fill the small white stone urn shown below. The pointed green ivy leaves are set beneath bright white ranunculus flower heads and buds. Following the circular shape I next placed green heads of *Viburnum opulus* and then white snowdrops complete the domed shape. The overall uniformity achieved is one of formality and so this arrangement could be used in many different ways, and would definitely be fitting at a wedding or any special celebration.

LEFT An elegant stone urn painted white contains a pleasing domed display of green *Viburnum opulus*, white ranunculus and snowdrops. The regular shape is created by using a foam ball as the base, and cutting the stems to 8cm. The density of the flowers means that this arrangement requires a large number of individual stems, so it is best created for a special occasion.

OPPOSITE An impressive display of double white lilac and green *Viburnum opulus*. A vase that narrows at the neck as this one does is perfect for supporting large splaying stems, while its bowl shape balances the flowers. Green and white flowers suit all decors and all age groups.

Even when fresh, many exotic varieties of flowers have an almost artificial look about them because of their sheer perfection and maybe because many have such a glossy sheen. Today all of these flowers are readily available year round from most good florists. Ours are, of course, brilliant replicas – all feel and look real; they are hand painted and would look glorious in any location. In the lovely tropical arrangement above, I placed coconut fibre inside the tall glass vase in which we have set three different colours and sizes of anthuriums, cream birds of paradise and their leaves, plus red phalaenopsis orchids and tall green grasses. We made this arrangement originally for a friend for her home in Barbados; she selected the flowers from the array she has growing in her garden there. In Barbados the phalaenopsis orchids grow naturally on the branch of a host tree, in a similar way that mistletoe grows as a parasite on trees in England. As long as my friend keeps the plant watered the orchids flower throughout the year.

Opposite are two complementary arrangements, one of artificial miniature oranges set on top of a round metal pot, the larger container made from reeded bamboo. I filled it with brilliantly coloured exotic flowers and rubbery green leaves. The five red banana flowers on their ridged stems carry immature bananas. The orange disa orchids sit beneath them and burnt orange birds of paradise are on the left. Disa orchids grow wild in South Africa, but are difficult to produce commercially.

Dried seed heads, fragile mouth-blown antique glass, rustic baskets, in fact almost any receptacle, can be used with artificial flowers because they do not need water. They can also stand anywhere without fear of water damage to precious surfaces. Containers can be ultra sophisticated, utterly wacky, completely traditional or just plain unusual. Let your imagination run wild!

OPPOSITE Purple and violet clematis flowers and leaves are supported in dry foam set inside a woven rattan basket. A generous abundance of floral material ensures the success of this design.

BELOW Two dried seed heads are planted with small phalaenopsis orchids. Real moss is bunched around the base of the flowers to hide the dry compost holding the stems in place.

using containers

Baskets have been used with flowers for many centuries as they are easily available and can be found in every home. The strikingly coloured vibrant purple clematis flowers and leaves opposite are set in a flared rattan basket and have a very natural feel. We use these clematis flowers extensively in many of our arrangements because the hand painting is extraordinarily good and they fit well with many of our containers. Standing behind the basket is a very old pine cupboard, hand painted with bunches of wheat – the country theme fits very well with the rustic basket. Always think of the setting before you decide which container will go where in your home.

Natural containers can have a more sophisticated feel. The huge dried seed heads shown left were collected from the Amazon basin, where they fall naturally to the ground when ripe. They have been hollowed out, making unusual containers for one pale pink and one white phalaenopsis orchid.

It is a strange truth that flowers tend to fit one type of container rather than another. I noticed one day a new designer who had not been to Ruckley before. She did not know what arrangements had previously been made, but she was using the same containers with the same flowers we had made time and again. She normally worked only with fresh flowers, which made the situation even more unusual. When we create new ranges for our mail order catalogue, we always source new containers first, otherwise it is incredibly difficult to think of new designs. Although the containers are no more important than the beautiful flowers we use, they are still a vital ingredient.

LEFT Clear glass vases cry out to be lined: the short stems on these bright pink double dahlias would have detracted from the fulsome effect created by the overlarge heads, so they have been hidden behind green leaves.

RIGHT I filled only one of these large black ceramic containers with purple clematis, orchids, rose flowers and buds and dark purple berries. The second empty vase is a counterpoint to the filled one, creating an interesting silhouette.

Some containers are so good looking that they are pieces of sculpture in their own right. To underline this fact, a design device I like to use is to group another – empty – container with one containing flowers. These lovely black highly glazed modern ceramic pots are in fact of two different sizes. The flowers have only been placed in the first vase and the second is there only for emphasis. The twining mass of dark purple flowers are an old English rose, a vanda orchid, rose buds, and a clematis vine, which is of a lighter shade of mauve. The vibrant colours of the flowers are reflected in the glaze of the vases, giving added impact. The sprawling shape of the arrangement reflects the natural habit of the roses and clematis.

Clear glass vases are indispensable to anyone who does any form of flower arranging, and most people have a selection of shapes and sizes in their cupboards. I find cubes especially versatile. The small glass cube above is lined with leaves, within which we have tightly packed bright pink double dahlias. Lining glass vases with leaves is an excellent way both to hide unsightly stems and add extra visual interest, but as an alternative to leaves, seed heads, fir cones, polished stone or plastic ice chips could be used. All of these add another dimension to simple arrangements in glass vases. They are particularly useful for hiding the dry foam or other fixing agents if you are creating more complex designs in glass containers. And there is no issue of water storage with fakes, so you don't have to use the vases set within a vase technique essential with fresh flowers.

Three glass cloches are used to cover 'growing' sage, thyme and basil – all would look charming in a kitchen. The cloches are copies of those made in Victorian times when they were used to force herbs to start growing earlier. Herbs were not as readily available in those days as they are today.

It is astonishing the difference the style of a container can make to the whole feel of an arrangement, even when the same flowers are used, as demonstrated by these very different treatments of amaryllis. Amaryllis have gained much popularity over the last few years and as fresh cut flowers they appear in our shops from early December. They are, however, extremely costly to produce and therefore to buy, so the beauty of our faux flowers is immediate – they are completely lifelike, last forever, and come in a huge range of colours similar to those of the fresh varieties.

For a large-scale arrangement I placed about half a dozen fake stems in a very tall glass vase, wrapped in a large exotic rubber leaf. The whole striking arrangement stands over a metre tall and works perfectly in an ultra-modern setting. The bottom of the stems are splayed open, as they do naturally when they have been in water for a few days – another lifelike touch.

As a contrast a 'growing' amaryllis was set in a plain terracotta pot. The bulb has the exact papery texture of the living bulb it replicates, and the leaves are intact. This setting is far more traditional than that shown opposite, illustrating the versatility of the genus. The vase to the right is hand made from white porcelain, which is encrusted with individual porcelain flowers and leaves. It is hard to know which is the most lovely – the flowers or the vase, but they fit together so well. The ivy completes the picture.

ABOVE Pure white amaryllis and trails of ivy are casually placed into a lovely porcelain vase that has been decorated with porcelain flowers. The arrangement, although modern in concept, could sit as easily in a traditional home.

LEFT Amaryllis flowers emerging from their own faux papery bulbs and set into pots with a little moss are indistinguishable from their real counterparts.

OPPOSITE Extra tall white amaryllis stems are wrapped in an exotic rubber leaf. Red amaryllis flowers have always been popular, especially for Christmas, but white ones are more versatile.

We are always being asked for arrangements that are linked or can be repeated – particularly for table decorations and more formal occasions such as weddings. Repeating identical items is used for emphasis and impact. Many different types of flowers can be used in this way, but smaller, simpler displays are generally more effective than large ones.

repeat designs

On a large table, especially a long rectangular one, it can be hard to achieve impact with floral displays without using large elaborate arrangements which then take up too much space and can block diners' sight lines. This is why repetition is such a useful design device. On the right three small purple phalaenopsis orchids are set in small glass spheres. Emphasis is achieved by simply repeating identical arrangements, as a single orchid could go unnoticed on a large table. I have used as many as 15 or 21 orchids on occasion, with great effect. A similar look would be achieved using several different colours of orchid, as long as they were placed in identical vases. I generally try to use flowers that are in season if possible. Orchids, however, can be used all year round, as they are almost always available.

In the winter everyone is delighted to see snowdrops appear and these 'growing' plants, left, set in moss, are very popular and so easy to replicate. A line of snowdrops on a mantelpiece or table looks wonderful even though they are so simple. We prefer to keep the snowdrops 'growing' out of their bulbs for a more realistic look and pack them tightly into the tiny glass cubes. One such plant on its own would look rather forlorn. Three would be okay – unless you are going for a symmetrical effect in any design odd numbers of things always work better than even ones – but the five here, unevenly spaced, really have impact. This is such a clean and fresh look. Repeat designs do not have to be linear: if you have five or more you can group them together in the centre of a round table.

Repetition often gives a very graphic effect, especially with tall, thin flowers. However it is possible to soften things. Mixing colours rather than using the same one is one way to go. Using low, looser, more delicate flower shapes can also be pretty. The pansies on the left have been placed on an afternoon tea table, and mix well with the pretty green and white floral tea set. How we wish the days of setting a quintessential English tea table were still with us – imagine cucumber sandwiches and toasted teacakes on a winter afternoon! The pansies are all of different colours, ranging from pink, to lavender, lemon and cream, but all sit in identical perfume bottles. We keep the stoppers and sometimes lay them beside their bottles, creating a casual feel. How inviting this all looks.

I varied the colours in the repeated roses, below, for a more naturalistic feel, and simply placed them in glass spheres. These fake roses are particularly lovely – each petal is curved and hand painted. This charming group would look lovely anywhere. You will notice that we have placed glass beads into the 'water', as we find that it is difficult to persuade the flower stems to stay in position in the water inside these pretty glass spheres. Glass beads are very helpful when using any glass bowls. If you are using real water then the vase can be filled to the top and so there is not a problem (provided you change the water before it discolours). The Stillwater™ resin is very expensive however, so we can use far less of it if we hold the flowers with beads or stones.

It is far simpler to put together fresh flowers of whatever colour than it is to mix up faux flowers. Somehow the huge variety of colours, texture and shading in fresh flowers allows them to blend together, but this is definitely not the case with their artificial brothers. In fact the dyeing and painting of our faux flowers is the most important part in their manufacture, and how we place them together is even more vital.

OPPOSITE An exceptionally lovely bowl of mixed roses, blossom and skimmia seeds. These flowers work well together because they share the same delicate pink and white shading.

BELOW An antique Chinese vase holding an array of peach roses. A large block of floral foam was cut to fit inside the vase first, to hold the flowers in position.

use of colour

PALE TONES   The roses and blossom on the opposite page describe perfectly the issues we face when matching colours and textures of artificial flowers. The roses are coated in wax after they have been through every other stage of painting and assembly. Waxing was first used in Victorian times on fresh roses to help preserve them for the winter season. The depth of colour achieved is extraordinarily good and they positively shine with vitality.

The peach roses, left, are displayed at various stages of opening, showing the differing depths of colour throughout their lives. An antique carved Chinese bowl enhances the delicacy of the peach colouring. The cream background does not detract from the simple beauty of the flowers. When selecting faux flowers for your own home a decision must be made as to whether the flowers are to startle and focus the eye, for example bright red flowers against a cream wall, or should you choose a softer shade to blend with your decor?

Colour is of paramount importance, but equally flowers without green leaves will never look real or natural. White flowers have a particular purity and clarity of their own, and are shown to perfection in the arrangement of camellias overleaf by the inclusion of the dark green foliage that enfolds them. I have

OPPOSITE David Austin™ Golden Celebrations roses with white snowberries and skimmia in a footed glass bowl. This arrangement would be perfect as a table decoration for a Golden Wedding anniversary dinner.

RIGHT White camellias, anemones, magnolia and skimmia nestle in a glass bowl. I love to place white flowers on or against dark wood, where they really stand out.

BELOW The colouring of these sunflowers, surrounded by leaves, is beautifully set off by the reeded vase. Sunflower heads are large enough to support themselves when used in abundance like this, so no other fixing, such as foam, is required.

placed them in a plain straight-sided glass bowl. At the front of the arrangement I set double white camellias surrounded by white *Magnolia* x *soulangeana,* and white anemones with black centres. Green skimmia adds the essential delicate background to the white flowers. Strands of contorted willow hold the flowers in the water.

A very important part of our collection is our range of David Austin™ roses. David is a neighbour and friend, and is the largest breeder of old English roses in the world today. A friend and I visited David's enormous rose garden one day, where the public can select their favourite rose bushes. My friend took hundreds of photographs and from these we developed with David a whole range of artificial copies of his beautiful real roses. In this picture we feature two varieties, Golden Celebrations and Teasing Georgia.

Shown left are some lovely golden sunflowers. The colouring of these is so realistic that we thought we must include them in this section. With my family, I have enjoyed so many wonderful holidays in France with sunflowers growing all around us, so they are yet another favourite of mine.

VIBRANT TONES To create a strong focal point in a room you need vibrant colours, and this is where the depth and strength of the colouration of the very best quality fake flowers really does come into its own. Below on this page is a striking glass bowl containing brilliantly hued summer flowers: peonies, sweetpeas, bougainvillea, tree peonies and roses. Even against a dark background, the strong colouring still emerges to great effect; it would create an even greater impact in a plain room. The different shapes and the diverse colours make this a most interesting arrangement.

On the right is a simpler hand-tied bunch of pink roses and berries. The vibrant colouring of the roses is wonderfully offset by the dark burgundy berries. The roses and berries do need to be hand tied before they are placed in the water otherwise the whole ensemble tends to collapse. (There are instructions for how to make a hand-tied arrangement on page 157.)

Sometimes using just one type of flower can work, especially when those flowers have impact. I tightly packed shocking pink amaryllis heads into an antique gilded porcelain vase, left, to enhance the stunning colour.

ABOVE This display of shocking pink amaryllis heads would work particularly well in a bedroom as it is such a romantic arrangement. Cut the stems short so that only the flower heads are on show.

RIGHT A glass bowl of herbaceous peonies, tree peonies, sweetpeas, bougainvillea, and burgundy roses. These stems are set in acrylic water, which gives a realistic effect, but is not vital to support the flowers.

OPPOSITE Bright pink roses are offset by burgundy berries. I used two different, but toning, colours in the roses. Hand-tied bouquets such as this one can easily be transferred from one vase to another for a change without disturbing the flowers themselves.

Colour, especially stronger tones, can be used to link different arrangements within the same room. These two pages emphasize varying shades of deep purple, through mauve to a hazy blue and burgundy pink. All these shades blend well together within the individual displays, the separate arrangements also creating three linked focal points. The display opposite, with purple passion flowers and sweetpeas, was placed on a coffee table. The purple ranunculus in the blue and white bowl are on the mantelpiece and the larger bowl of blue and purple clematis flowers, below, were situated on a sunny windowsill. So the vibrant colours draw the eye into three separate locations. The cushions on the sofa are the only other colour-linked item.

This range of colours works extremely well within a modern white based decor. However, different colours would be needed in, say, a seaside home or a rural cottage. In other words, awareness of outside influences plays a huge part in selection of flowers for a room, be it the countryside, the city lights, a river or green fields – each situation will suggest a different palette.

ABOVE A blue and white porcelain bowl holds blowsy flower heads of deep and lighter toned purple ranunculus and clematis. Hold each flowering stem against the side of the vase to judge the correct length before you cut it.

RIGHT A glass bowl of purple and lilac coloured clematis flowers and leaves, with richly toned anemones tucked among them.

OPPOSITE A charmingly straggling arrangement, with two shades of mauve and purple passion flowers and sweetpeas in blue and burgundy, is set in a simple tall glass square bud vase. Faux flower stems are pliable and will maintain whatever form you give them: simply bend them into a shape that looks natural and works with the other flowers in the arrangement.

How many of us buy a beautiful fresh pot plant and kill it either by over or under watering within a few weeks? I know that I do this, particularly with plants such as poinsettias at Christmas. All the plants shown in this section 'live' happily on and do not mind suffering total neglect – they will look glorious for many years to come.

OPPOSITE Using appropriate containers is essential to convey the impression of a real living plant. These tall white foxgloves are planted in a convincingly weathered large terracotta pot.

BELOW LEFT Attention to detail both in the manufacture of the plant material and in the construction of the finished object ensure that the beauty of this white slipper orchid will endure.

planted designs

At home at Ruckley we use many artificial potted plants, particularly in the summer when they stand happily outside on a terrace. They need some protection in inclement weather, but I find the odd shower of rain does very little harm to them. Strong winds however are far more likely to cause damage.

One year at the Chelsea Flower Show in London huge pots of real white foxgloves were everywhere. The wonderful replicas on the right are copies – the whole construction is as near a perfect copy as it is possible to be. Even the 'soil' they are 'growing' in looks perfect – it is a composite set with clear glue, giving the texture of real earth. The terracotta pot has a slight haze of green moss covering part of the base, to give the appearance of a pot that has stood outdoors. The whole display is enormous (about 160cm tall) and staggeringly realistic. So often people touch the flowers and the soil and look puzzled!

On the left is a sweet white slipper orchid, with delicately arching flower sprays as if reaching for the sunlight pouring through the window. The green glossy leaves and the strong white roots add authenticity to this lovely plant. Many different species of orchid and plants are potted in this way in our factory, using a large assortment of pots and containers – I think their popularity is due partly to the beauty of the plants and partly to the lack of attention required in their maintenance. They are a quick and sure way of dressing any room in any house and lend an instant charm. The only problem is that if a neighbour has been asked to look after your house when you are away, so often that person will water the artificial plants!

The huge display of pink magnolia 'growing' in a black container covered with polished stones opposite is one of our favourite and most striking arrangements – maybe because magnolia flowers are so often killed by late frosts, so some years it is impossible to enjoy any magnolia at all in the home.

Fresh orchids have an enviably long flowering time, but it can be tricky to persuade them to re-flower year after year, and they make pretty unappealing specimens with no flowers in evidence. It would take a very talented orchid grower to grow a real specimen as bountiful as the cascade of white phalaenopsis orchids left, in a highly glazed turquoise bowl.

The deep pink peony plant below, about 160cm tall, is also extraordinarily beautiful. It looks as though it has just been transplanted from a greenhouse – the flowers are at varying stages of development, from tight buds to fully open. The light streaming through the conservatory window brings the whole plant to life. The flowering time of peonies is very short, so how wonderful, then, to enjoy this lovely plant throughout the year.

ABOVE When it comes to creating convincing living plants, it is realistic touches, such as the bamboo support canes and arterial roots on these white phalaenopsis orchids, that make the real difference.

RIGHT This bush of bright pink peonies in a terracotta pot has a wonderfully naturalistic arching shape.

OPPOSITE I love the gleaming black finish of the polished black bowl and pebbles that this magnificent magnolia sits in. It has a subtle oriental feel that feels very appropriate for this plant.

RIGHT Spring flowers call for appropriately rustic containers, such as this charming woven wicker basket and small terracotta pot both holding glowing white hyacinths.

OPPOSITE This selection of spring flowers set in small rattan containers with moss are frozen in a particularly beautiful stage of their development. With real flowers this display would be over in just a few days. These can be grouped together as here or displayed on their own.

BELOW The addition of a vintage-style glass cloche transforms a simple blue drumstick primula set in moss into a miniature work of art.

Potted spring plants are always so popular, as they appear in our shops before the actual plants arrive in our gardens – they are such harbingers of things to come. The blue *Primula denticulata* left are delightful under their glass Victorian cloches. To construct something similar, I would suggest you glue some dry foam onto a flat white plate, simply insert the plant and then cover the foam with moss. The glass cloche is then placed over the entire arrangement as a finishing touch. This is so simple to make but so pretty.

On the opposite page we have three linked arrangements set in unusual rattan containers. The flowers used are white tulips, pale yellow daffodils and paper white narcissus. All are emerging out of their natural bulbs. These are faux flowers so they can sit happily on any surface without the need for a mat to absorb water spillages. They can be left in situ for many months until spring gives way to summer. Those archetypal heralds of spring, hyacinths, do need a spray of perfume to bring them to life. Seen growing in a casual rattan basket (above) these glowing white flowers are a delight to the eye. All the hyacinths are at varying stages of opening. The simple terracotta pot is there just as a charming echo to the main arrangement.

All of these potted items give joy and are suitable for any interior decor, or situation, whether it be a formal room, an office, a hotel reception area, or a bedroom. Also, just think how delightful to open a door into a room that is little used and to see these wonderful spring flowers 'growing'.

Greenery and grasses are now high fashion in the plant world! All gardening books and magazines feature more and more informal gardens incorporating many species of grasses and green plants such as hostas, rather than just high-maintenance flowers. Italian gardens are also enjoying a renaissance, so small topiary trees, including rosemary, olive and box, are very popular.

OPPOSITE Potted herbs – basil, mint, rosemary – are lined up together with a small olive topiary tree and, in the background, a pot of sage.

BELOW A box topiary tree in a terracotta pot. Box is often associated with formal styling, so the naturalistic shape of this standard is unusual and refreshing.

greenery and grasses

It is only in recent years that such a large selection of fresh herbs have been readily available in supermarkets. Perhaps this is due to the present interest in Italian food, and indeed for all herbs that are needed for recipes from around the world – hence our replicas are also in great demand. How realistic they look – but please do remember not to break off a sprig of basil to use in your cooking!

Green comes in many varieties: the selection of herbs on the right shows the many different shades of this colour to great effect. Pictured 'growing' in terracotta pots with antiqued copper labels are herbs such as sage, basil, mint, and rosemary. The tall olive topiary tree adds height and extra interest to the group. These would look equally attractive sitting on a kitchen windowsill or table. All of these plants have been copied from their real brothers, hence they are not too perfect, which adds to their realism.

The delicate box topiary, opposite, sits sweetly in its terracotta pot. This would look lovely in a conservatory and could be used casually for an outdoor picnic table. It could also be effective as a repeat design, such as those featured on pages 34–37. Conservatories are very challenging spaces for living plants. Temperatures range from too high to too low and make caring for them extremely difficult and time consuming. It is also expensive to heat or cool a conservatory to maintain an ambient temperature just for the survival of your plants! All these planted designs could sit happily in a conservatory, on a patio in the summer months, or in a living room.

RIGHT A natural rustic wreath with pine branches and large bleached fir cones. The circular nature of wreaths ensures that as a design device they always add a sense of movement. You can buy plastic-backed floral foam rings, into which you can easily push the firm stems of faux flowers and greenery.

OPPOSITE These two handmade over-sized glass containers, with their arching bunches of wild grasses, stand at just over 120cm tall.

BELOW What could be simpler? These delicate green ferns standing in a glass vase are just so pretty. To create a similar upward shape from individual stems of foliage, you can bind the base of the stems with twine before placing them in a vase.

The very large uncomplicated arrangements shown opposite contain natural bunches of bronze-tinged grasses with their fluffy seed heads. The glass jars are enormous and almost too heavy to lift, and each one is signed by the artist who made them. In the bottom of each of them we have placed some dried seed heads, or rosecones, to echo the colour of the grasses. They are photographed against an old sandstone wall with a book of old flower paintings, but would look equally at home in a modern conservatory. Duplicating the same arrangement adds emphasis to the design.

The picture above shows a table against the same sandstone wall, on which we have placed a very large natural wreath using bleached fir cones and green pine branches. The trailing pale green amaranthus stems add brightness, as they catch the light. This wreath would be fine to display throughout the year, but at Christmas, by adding baubles or poinsettia flowers, it could be adapted to fit into the festive season. We use wreaths extensively throughout the year, sometimes hanging on doors, but usually as a table centre around a glass cylinder vase containing a tall candle.

Lastly I placed some simple fern leaves into a plain glass vase. They stand about a metre tall and have a very clean graceful elegance that helps to bring together the other decorative elements in a room.

four ways with roses

The shading of the petals on this delightful old English rose, above, from very pale on the outside to a much stronger colour in the centre, is a truly remarkable representation of its type. I used similar roses in all these arrangements, as well as spray roses and the larger hybridized type.

The small rose posies sitting in the wire candelabra have not been set in Stillwater™ resin but are just placed in each vase. A few small roses have been left on the table to add a natural touch. The vases can then be reused with different seasonal flowers, such as poinsettias at Christmas, or snowdrops in springtime. I also use this candelabra with small tealight candles. The four linked vases of garden roses feature different species, but toning colours. This idea works well in a room that is seldom used, such as a guest bedroom, or at a time when garden roses are not available.

The summer wreath is made using pink cabbage roses, all fully open, together with green and pink hydrangea heads. The dark green rose and hydrangea leaves add emphasis – a gentle spray of rose perfume will give delight throughout the summer. This arrangement looks equally attractive laid flat as a centrepiece with a glass cylinder vase. The lantern offers protection from breezes or light winds, so the arrangement can be used outside. The beautiful large bowl of summer roses and other flowers, as if picked from your garden, is a very natural arrangement.

OPPOSITE PAGE: TOP LEFT An enormous white iron urn 'planted' with cream vanda orchids. Indistinguishable from real orchids, this huge display is much admired on my terrace.

TOP RIGHT Orchid heads can also be used for low arrangements. These white cattleya orchids with orange-red centres are set in a footed glass bowl.

BOTTOM LEFT Sprays of white phalaenopsis orchids, edged with mauve, in a small porcelain rice bowl topped with moss is a classically clean design.

BOTTOM RIGHT Orchids do not just come in white, as this arching stem of bright green phalaenopsis flowers amply demonstrate.

LEFT A cream vanda orchid head, which is hand painted, showing perfect details.

four ways with orchids

What a high-fashion flower orchids have become, available everywhere as plants or as cut flowers. Their popularity as faux flowers is extraordinary. We use only very realistic fakes, indistinguishable from the real thing. I often think what a huge help these are to interior designers, allowing them to leave the rooms they have decorated beautifully finished with the flowers they recommend.

On my stone patio in summer I like to display these lovely vanda orchids, 'growing' naturally in a large white cast-iron urn. I would not recommend that they remain outside all year, but they will withstand light showers of summer rain. The worst problem if using artificial flowers outside is wind, so I always bring them indoors in the autumn. The sheer weight of this heavy cast iron urn ensures that light winds do not affect them too seriously. Much smaller in scale are the white cattleya orchids, featured top right. They have orangey-red centres and such pretty leaves and are shown set with Stillwater™ resin in a footed glass bowl, ideal to sit on a coffee table, or by a bedside. Equally petite is a sweet, but tiny, bowl of phalaenopsis orchids seated in foam covered with rich, green moss.

The glowing green phalaenopsis orchid, placed in an intricate amber glass perfume bottle, is surrounded by matching glass baubles and a gilded shell. The light shining through the petals reveals the intricate veining of the orchid, and the light on the amber glass is quite lovely.

spring flowers

spring flower gallery

Flowers epitomize spring – the most
joyous of seasons. In this section we show you a small
selection from the enormous variety produced by
mother nature. In my own garden daffodils, snowdrops,
fritillaria, crocus, aconites, perennial tulips, garlic
flowers and bluebells all flourish in the wilder wooded
areas. Hybridized tulips, another of the spring keynote
flowers, are perhaps slightly different in that they can
look out of place in an untamed, naturalistic setting,
unlike the earlier flowering spring flowers. The tulips
we feature overleaf are mostly May flowering, and very
tall, so are impressive growing in a more formal garden
setting, in pots or among the flower beds.

Among our spring collection of faux flowers are
many bare branches, including catkins and pussy
willow, which help enormously when arranging flowers
such as daffodils. They support tall leggy flowers and
give a more structured look when needed. They are also
helpful when making hand-tied bunches and
sometimes we make whole arrangements using nothing
but pussy willow standing in tall vases. They are very
popular as they remind people of the bunches they used
to collect from the hedgerows.

CLOCKWISE FROM TOP LEFT A dark burgundy parrot tulip. A yellow pointed lily-flowered tulip with lovely black stamens. A common round tulip beautifully painted in shades of peach. A white pointed lily-flowered tulip with black and yellow stamens.

tulips

Here is a large close-up of a wonderfully hand-painted parrot tulip that is quite extraordinarily beautiful. While looking through some ancient books at the Royal Horticultural Society's Lindley Library in London, I came across an amazing picture, painted between 1720 and 1730 by August Wilhelm Sievert showing an almost identical tulip – he must have been painting at the height of 'tulip mania' in Holland.

How wonderful, after the drab short days of winter, when the days gradually lengthen and the spring bulbs start to appear. The bright colours are both inspirational and energizing. Gone are the long dark evenings, and we can again fill our homes with lovely spring flowers.

OPPOSITE Two small white china jugs filled with a variety of different coloured daffodils. These casual bunches are designed to look as though the flowers have just been picked in the garden and simply placed on a dressing table.

BELOW Two repeat designs of yellow tulips, varied in height for extra interest. Some have bent heads so that they appear more natural. Real tulips develop that characteristic arching shape in a vase because the stems continue to grow after they have been cut.

spring flowers in the home

It is rarely necessary to make formal arrangements using spring flowers – often a casual look is more successful, maybe because so many of them were originally found growing wild in woodlands, their natural habitat. They are, of course, now produced commercially on a huge scale. This sense of abundance, so welcome after the leaner winter months, can be reflected in vibrant and colourful artificial arrangements all around the home.

Surely the first messenger of spring is the snowdrop. Appearing just as winter is losing its icy grip, it is perhaps the most welcome of all sights. Snowdrops are such simple flowers to arrange, and we have featured them as a linked design on page 34. Next in the seasonal display come daffodils. They too are very easy to arrange – a bunch of daffodils cannot fail to cheer and add instant brightness to our lives and homes.

In my garden I find growing tulips from year to year a complete nightmare – we plant hundreds, they flower wonderfully, but the following year just one or two diseased and dispirited plants appear. I have now discovered that the older breeds of tulips will survive if they are planted at least 20cm deep. So this year I will wait with bated breath to see if this is true. It is such a lot of work to plant so many bulbs each year, how wonderful it will be if they can naturalize and appear year after year, just as reliably as my fake ones make their reappearance in my home year after year! I used two square glass vases to link the arrangements shown left. Both are packed with differing shades of yellow tulip.

THIS PAGE A stunning basket packed with bluebells, tulips, crocus and narcissus: this arrangement makes me think of a spring garden in miniature.

OPPOSITE Graceful sprays of peach aquilegias are set into resin, to replicate water, in a glass vase. Remove any foliage from the stems below the resin level.

A lot of my favourite spring flower displays rely on using just one flower variety in an arrangement. However I do like to mix varieties as well, to demonstrate just how bountiful nature is at this time of year. In the rattan basket opposite is a selection of spring flowers – including crocus, narcissus, pink and yellow tulips and bluebells – with some dark green ivy leaves for contrast. How lovely they look; the colours are jewel bright and can only inspire a feeling of happiness. This is such a simple arrangement to make – place dry foam into the bottom of the basket, cut the flowers to fairly short varying lengths and insert them into the foam. Moss has been added to hide the dry foam.

The peachy pink coloured aquilegias above are sitting next to a basin to add a decorative element in a bathroom. Faux flowers can cope with steamy atmospheres more happily than real flowers do. Although simple in design, this is the sort of arrangement of which I never tire – the flowers are beautifully painted and the stems and leaves are delicate and delightful.

LEFT The stems of the massed burgundy and white fritillarias in this footed glass vase are supported by the woody stems of pussy willow and softened with the fronds of green ferns.

OPPOSITE These hand-painted parrot tulips are simply arranged in two different glass vases. The artistry that goes into reproducing the elaborate markings – mutations caused by virus in real tulips – I find incredible.

BELOW Tall stems of peach blossom in a white ceramic vase. Large floor-standing arrangements such as these become a real talking point in a room.

Real blossom lasts only hours after it has been picked – how wonderful therefore to have the option of enjoying these faux replicas for much longer. The peach blossom shown right stands about 1.5m high and is pictured brightening up the corner of a room. At the top of the stems you can see the pale green leaves emerging, just as they would on real flowering stems. The vase is white porcelain encrusted with hand-made porcelain flowers. The flowers have not been set into the vase with resin, so that when blossom is out of season, other varieties can be used.

The two tulip arrangements opposite are placed in a kitchen – waiting to be taken into the living room? Or are they to stay in the kitchen? They would be happy anywhere. The small arrangement is a single tulip in a cut-glass perfume bottle, while the larger cylinder vase holds a dozen longer stems. If you are making something similar at home, then slightly bending the heads helps to make the design look natural. The light shining through the window shows each petal beautifully.

Sometimes it is possible to be much more generous with fake flowers than one would be with their natural counterparts. I love seeing carpets of fritillaries in woodland, but I would never dream of cutting them from the wild. Commercially grown fritillaries are quite hard to come by, have a limited season and can be very expensive. How wonderful then to enjoy such a fulsome display of fake ones.

Purple, lilac and white coloured ranunculus in a glass bowl with contorted willow stems set in the vase. The domed shape of the flowers is echoed by the globe-like glass vase.

One of our most popular flowers, all year round, is ranunculus, but it is especially nice to see it in spring, its natural flowering season. We have them in many different colours and shades, ranging from purple, through pink to orange, yellow and white. The original flowers, before they were hybridized, were always yellow and I have seen many flowering on the banks of Scottish rivers while I have been fishing. Kingcups and buttercups are both members of the *Ranunculae* family. As well as cut flowers for the home, the real varieties are also available as potted plants for use outside. The purple, lilac and white ranunculus opposite are held in place using lengths of contorted willow. Firstly I made a hand-tied bunch of the ranunculus to hold the domed shape of the flowers. The twisted willow was pushed into the bowl, followed by the hand-tied ranunculus.

White arrangements are by far the most versatile, as they can be placed almost anywhere in any home. They brighten up a dark corner and catch any available light – always fresh looking and appealing to all. On the right we have a white camellia with leaves and buds standing in a cut glass vase, pictured on a dressing table where they will be enjoyed everyday. The problem with these early flowering camellias is always the risk of frost, so their faux counterparts are particularly useful.

These pretty white freesias are excellent replicas, and look best when simply displayed in a plain glass vase. Again a small spray of perfume would add delight. Freesias are one of our best-selling flowers, reflecting the popularity of the real ones. We have these in many colours, and we often use them in repeat designs, either all of one colour, or one of each colour.

ABOVE RIGHT This romantic little arrangement has such an artless charm: a white camellia with buds and leaves in a cut glass vase

BELOW RIGHT White freesias in a simple glass vase are placed on a bright bedroom windowsill. Many people do not like sleeping in the same room as fresh flowers, but fake flowers can be used anywhere.

RIGHT A table beautifully set for a spring wedding using lily of the valley, or *Convallaria majalis*, as the key flower. Its meaning is 'You will find happiness' so it is a particularly appropriate choice for the start of anyone's married life.

spring wedding

Many brides electing to get married in spring choose one type of flower to set the theme. This can look very smart. There are so many different flowers that could be used at this time of year, but at the moment lilies of the valley are the most popular. They are a classic favourite; their delicacy lends themselves to pretty styling on the rest of the table and they set a very romantic tone. Using artificial flowers on the table, rather than fresh, is a huge bonus, as all can be prepared beforehand – all the flowers remain brilliantly white, with no brown dying flowers in sight. We do make a lily perfume, so a gentle spray would add to the realism.

The lilies of the valley used in the centrepiece for this table setting stand in a lovely crystal cut glass bowl. The flowers have been stripped of their leaves and massed into the vase. Dry foam could easily be used here as long as it was covered with moss. Each of the tall glass candelabras hold smaller, hand-tied posies of lily of the valley and included sprays of clematis leaves, which are smaller than lily leaves and easier to manage.

Individual small sprays have been placed on top of the napkins – some are tied with lace ribbon and some with green velvet. Dotted around the table are small perfume bottles containing five stems of the lilies, and a slightly larger simple glass cylinder, also containing the flowers. Using many small vases, rather than one large arrangement, adds far more interest to the table setting, and contributes to the pretty, feminine look.

To make the tied bunch in the cylinder vase pictured opposite, take some round dry foam and a small bunch of lilies and leaves. Wrap each flower stem in the foliage and arrange these around the foam, then bind tightly with twine. Push a few more stems of flowers and leaves into the centre of the foam. A simpler version can be made if leaves are tied horizontally onto the foam.

When using faux flowers for a wedding, life becomes far easier for the bride and her mother. All floral preparation can be completed beforehand, so removing last-minute panics. Sometimes the flowers that the bride particularly wants are not available fresh at that time, or only at a vastly inflated price. All of the big international wholesalers and flower markets increase their prices at those times when they know demand will be at its greatest, such as Mother's Day, Easter or Valentine's Day. If your wedding day falls around those times, you will inevitably end up paying more for fresh flowers. Using faux flowers will enable you to fix your budget well in advance.

ABOVE AND RIGHT For the napkin decorations, single sprays of lily of the valley are tied with either lace (for the female guests) or green velvet (for the gentlemen). It is personal touches such as this that make the table setting extra special.

OPPOSITE One of the many different small arrangements used on the wedding table: a small hand-tied bunch of lily of the valley set in a small glass cylinder vase. The flower stems are wrapped in the lily foliage and then inserted into foam.

easter breakfast

For me, Easter is a time for family. It is a somehow more relaxed holiday than Christmas, so before the excitement of our annual Easter egg hunt, there is time to start the day with a wonderfully indulgent, leisurely breakfast. And if Easter falls late in the year and the weather proves kind, why not set up outside and enjoy the spring sunshine? Our table is set on a south-facing terrace, but the decorations and arrangements would be just as happy sitting on the kitchen or dining room table, if the weather is less accommodating.

The flower displays on our Easter table are original and highly decorative. Eight large white ostrich eggs have been glued together, so that they support each other, and simply filled with a selection of bluebells, jonquils, daffodils and muscari, or grape hyacinths. None of the flowers has been set permanently into the eggs, so that they can easily be removed and replaced with summer, or other seasonal, flowers. You need to use at least two, but better yet three ostrich eggs to make the centrepiece, otherwise the eggs fall over. It is also helpful if someone else holds the eggs upright for you while you glue them together.

LEFT An individual Easter ostrich egg arrangement. As well as looking so pretty on the table, it can be fun to give these to friends and family as an alternative to chocolate eggs on Easter day.

OPPOSITE ABOVE Pink and white tinged muscari with a few bluebells are grouped in a small white jug. The delicacy of the flowers is a perfect complement to the fine china used in the table setting.

OPPOSITE BELOW Here just a few of the muscari are included in a larger bunch of bluebells in a glass vase. The repetition of the bluebells in differing quantities in all of the arrangements helps to pull together all of the floral decoration.

As well as the eight ostrich eggs glued together to form the centrepiece, I have included some single eggs, also holding spring flowers. To keep them in position I set them onto double-sided tape on a small plate. I just love the way the slanting morning sunlight catches the glaze of the small green teapot.

Other floral decorations include a pretty china jug casually filled with more muscari. The cups and saucers are very delicate (as are the eggs themselves) and are hand painted with pictures of spring flowers. The antique silver bowl of salt is ready for use with the real breakfast eggs. Elsewhere on the table is a glass vase filled with 'just gathered' bluebells and muscari, with just a few green leaves. Placed together, blue and yellow flowers are a delight.

Of all the wild flowers growing at Ruckley, bluebells are my favourite. Intermingled with the bluebells are carpets of garlic flowers and the brilliant blue mixed with the white is a feast for the eyes. How fortunate we are to have so many wild areas left – they are havens for birds, flowers and animals.

summer flowers

OPPOSITE, CLOCKWISE FROM TOP LEFT Multicoloured annual sweetpeas – our fake varieties are as popular as fresh ones. A glowing white casablanca lily – a gentle spray of lily perfume makes them indistinguishable from real lilies. A bright pink gerbera, showing its daisy-like shape. The delicate shading on this herbaceous peony is all hand painted.

THIS PAGE The slight yellowing of the outer leaves on this giant-headed sunflower is a very realistic touch.

PREVIOUS PAGES At Ruckley we grow so much lavender, mostly 'Hidcote Blue', and it is alive with bees and butterflies throughout the flowering season. These bunches are so realistic you would almost expect to see the bees investigating them!

summer flower gallery

English gardens are filled with flowers – roses, peonies, delphiniums, lavender, honeysuckle and lilies, to name but a few – all redolent of warm summer days. Now our wonderful replicas can fill our homes with flowers that look as if we had just picked them from the garden. With so many summer flowers to choose from, it has been difficult to select just a few for this gallery. We must start, however, with sweetpeas as they are our out and out best seller. With their delicate heads and their wonderful range of colours, it is hardly surprising how popular they are. They make a superb flower to choose for a wedding. Next we have wonderful white lilies – again the perfect flower for a summer wedding. The huge advantage is that the stamens can be left in the centre of the faux flowers without the problem of pollen stains. This stunning Sarah Bernhardt double herbaceous peony is perhaps my favourite. At home I grow so many varieties of peonies – the mostly highly prized being the huge-headed tree variety; which I have in a deep burgundy pink. Gerberas are enormously versatile flowers. The flower head shown here is a close-up of one of those shown in a table setting on pages 2 to 3.

roses On the right is a hybrid Ecuadorean pale peach rose. In Ecuador the real roses grow to enormous sizes because of the height at which they are grown. The stem length is also impressive, making them instantly recognizable.

OPPOSITE, CLOCKWISE FROM TOP LEFT We show here a few of the many roses that we produce. A peach-yellow Old English rose, showing curving petals and a great depth of colour. A more open type, this shows the changing stages of colouring achieved as the rose slowly unfurls. This is a moss rose spray in deep burgundy with wonderful detailing on the stems. This delicious pink half open bud has been perfectly painted to emulate the slight browning of the outside petals.

With the huge abundance of fresh flowers in the summer months, you might feel there is less need to rely on faux flowers. However, even though so many fresh varieties are available, life is still much easier if you use fake ones, leaving your garden intact and you with more time.

summer flowers in the home

Many of us do not in any case have access to garden flowers, and even if we do it always seems a pity to pick them. Very few people actually have a patch in their garden which is just for picking. In Victorian times, gardeners working in large country houses always kept a dedicated area which was actually called the picking garden. Nowadays this would be a rare luxury.

What glory summer flowers can bring to the home with their stunning colours and impressive forms. The tall glass vase opposite is full of peonies and sweetpeas – a wonderful array of flowers that look just as though they were gathered from the garden. The range of pinks is as accurate as those growing outside. The large double peonies give boldness whilst the sweetpeas add a lighter touch. The sharp green of the *Viburnum opulus* adds depth to the design. The background is simple; the white blinds highlight the flowers.

The peonies in the smaller picture are placed in a blue-and-white jug against a pale blue background. Similar varieties of peonies have been used to those in the glass vase opposite and again they are at varying stages of opening. The short flowering season for fresh peonies is always disappointing, so what joy to have these in our homes for longer, without rain damage, falling petals and unpleasant water in the vase. I have a passion for blue-and-white porcelain, probably because I travel in China so often. This jug is an inexpensive reproduction, but no less beautiful because of that. Peonies and roses always look lovely in this sort of vase – it is a look that has been popular for many centuries.

OPPOSITE One of the joys of summer flowers is their height. This enormous vase is filled with huge blue delphiniums and a selection of grasses.

RIGHT Two different glasses of sweetpeas; one with mixed colours and the other with just blue flowers. Both these small arrangements would be ideal for use on a table at parties or weddings, or indeed anywhere around the home.

BELOW The blue of agapanthus is such an unusual shade – almost electric blue. Pushing some stems of trailing ivy into the base of the arrangement helps convey the idea of a living plant.

Delphiniums were inspirational in starting my dried flower company. I have always loved them and used to dry many from my garden by hanging them over the Aga cooker. Eventually, when I needed more for the business, I contacted a seed merchant in Holland and spent a fortune buying F1 hybrid delphinium seeds. The acres of flowers were extraordinary, ranging in colour from white, through pink to deepest blue – quite breathtaking. Sadly because the flowers were all growing outside in the field, they all cross pollinated the following year, and although still magical, the colours, of course, had not stayed true. When I came to start my fake flower business I had to have delphiniums and they too are magnificent. Grasses have been added to the vase of elegant flowers. This arrangement has been selected by the Royal Horticultural Society in London for the excellence of the flowers.

Sweetpeas are undoubtedly one of the joys of summer. But growing your own requires constant – almost daily – attention to prevent seed pods from forming and to encourage continual flowering. And I find it hard to cut straight stems of a uniform length to display in my home. These fake ones have all of the charm of fresh ones, without the effort involved. In the larger glass I placed a single coloured bunch of blue stems, alongside a smaller glass using many colours, a look more typical of garden flowers. The blue agapanthus is potted and stands against a conservatory wall.

Roses, of course, are now available all year round, and are sourced by the big international plant markets from as far afield as South America and South Africa to ensure a constant supply. However, to me they are still essentially a summer flower, particularly the many varieties of English roses. The two shown above are exact replicas of Teasing Georgia and Golden Celebrations, displayed together as the colours of these two yellow roses complement each other so well. These are David Austin™ roses, bred by my friend and neighbour David Austin. The roses sit very happily in this lovely turquoise heavily glazed bowl, and I've placed other ceramic pieces – a jug and small bowl – nearby to complete the composition.

The green herbs and leaves are sitting happily waiting to be 'used' on a sunny shelf. Green leaves, herbs and grasses are such a fashion statement at the moment in floristry – the naturalness of the containers makes these arrangements ideal for a windowsill or kitchen shelf.

I have had such happy holidays in France with my family and have wonderful memories of being entirely surrounded by fields of brightly coloured sunflowers, as shown opposite. It is indeed true that they all face in one direction, but they do not actually turn their heads to follow the sun. This was a surprising discovery. In the arrangement the flowers are all of different varieties in varying shades and sizes – the larger blooms have darker centres, adding interest. How perfectly they light up this kitchen setting.

ABOVE LEFT A scattering of fallen petals around the base of the vase add authenticity to this display of David Austin™ roses.

ABOVE RIGHT Casual containers – glass jars tied with twine – hold mixed bunches of herbs and green leaves, including variegated hostas. This is a great way of creating a temporary display from stems left over from other displays.

OPPOSITE A naïve hand-thrown terracotta jug, holding a bright bunch of yellow sunflowers, with a single stem held in a glass vase standing at its base.

OPPOSITE Tall spires of white foxgloves, viburnum and ferns will remain cool looking, however hot the weather.

RIGHT This to me is the perfect marriage of container with flower: white wisteria and leaves are displayed in a green vase embossed with matching white flowers.

BELOW Gardening with no hard work involved: a huge arrangement of a 'growing' hydrangea plant.

Hot summer weather can play havoc with fresh flowers: higher temperatures mean they will last for an even shorter time than usual. Fake flowers will remain completely unaffected, however high the mercury rises or the humidity increases. In warmer weather it is nice to introduce a fresh note in your home, and I find myself drawn to cool white and green colour schemes in these situations. A casual country arrangement, opposite, redolent of hedgerows or of armfuls of flowers picked on a woodland walk, sets the tone perfectly. White foxgloves, fresh green viburnum and large fronds of ferns are casually placed in a rustic terracotta jug. Surprisingly the white foxgloves stand out remarkably well against the white blinds.

Another green and white arrangement – this time using long skeins of white wisteria with fresh leaves – stands in a tall green and white heavily glazed and hand painted terracotta vase. The whole ensemble is well over a metre tall, and stands on a white painted wooden floor. I think this could be a very useful

arrangement in either a modern or traditional setting. Real white wisteria with its long racemes of gloriously scented flowers grows all over the back of our home. It is much later to flower than the mauve variety, and the flowers and leaves both appear together, as they do in these hand-made stems.

These exquisite palest pink hydrangeas 'growing' in a large terracotta pot, sit happily in the sunlight on this patio. It is virtually impossible to distinguish these faux flowers from their real counterpart. The pot has been slightly mossed – has it just been brought from the greenhouse? Light summer rain will not affect these flowers, but they must be under cover in more severe weather. No watering is required, so no need to worry when you go on holiday. The flowers themselves have the natural papery feel of slightly dehydrated hydrangeas.

summer wedding

Could anything be more romantic than this garden setting for a summer wedding? In the background is an old ballustraded stone wall, with dahlias and roses naturally growing in the borders. Who would ever guess that the flowers on the table are actually artificial?

The main flower colour is white, and white roses were the key flower requested by the bride, so the table centre is a ring of white roses, both open and in bud, with jasmine, hyacinths and lily of the valley also included. In the centre of the ring is a cylinder vase containing a white candle. To vary the height on the table, I also included a very tall-stemmed Champagne glass containing trailing white wisteria and leaves.

Ordinary folding chairs were dressed to match the table with voluminous lengths of pure white muslin. The fabric was gathered in generous folds at the back and held in place with a single white rose, highlighted by dark green leaves. The same single rose detail is echoed on the top of the wedding cake, a single layer tied with lace ribbon. This is a very simple idea but it continues the white rose theme and looks extremely elegant.

LEFT The bridal bouquet, which was hand tied and bound with white silk ribbon to match the flowers, contains roses, jasmine, cow parsley, lily of the valley, hyacinths and ivy.

OPPOSITE The decorations include a central wreath around a candle, a taller vase, roses on the chair backs and a large pedestal arrangement to one side. The blend of faux flowers in and around the table with all the fresh flowers in the garden is seamless.

BELOW Continuing the all-white theme, the same flower types used for the bride's bouquet are used in the central arrangement.

How much easier and stress free all of this is to achieve using artificial flowers, rather than the complications of ordering fresh roses and other flowers. The bride and her mother can arrive relaxed and happy knowing all will be in good order and just as they left it to get ready for the big occasion.

Standing near the table is a floor-standing pedestal in the shape of a large glass Champagne coupe to reflect the smaller Champagne glasses on the table. This pedestal arrangement could easily have been transferred from the church, or wedding venue, to the reception following the service, ensuring that the flowers can be enjoyed for longer. As well as roses, hyacinths, sweetpeas and lily of the valley it also contains frothy cow parsley and trailing ivy.

The bride's bouquet has also been brought from the wedding service and laid on the table. We also made a similar smaller version for the bridesmaid, using identical flowers to those for the bride with the exception of using rose buds rather than full blown roses to better suit the scale of the bouquet.

The whole of this table setting would look equally beautiful if the wedding was inside instead of in our lovely English garden.

RIGHT A summer lunch party situated on a covered outside terrace takes as its decorative theme roses in all their glory.

BELOW The centrepiece for the table shows the breathtaking variety – and beauty – of faux roses.

al fresco lunch

This is such a pretty setting for a summer lunch party, undercover, but allowing extensive views of the garden. I really enjoy using fake flowers for outdoor decoration: what better demonstration of the quality of contemporary faux flowers than the fact that they do not jar at all when placed among their natural counterparts, but merge seamlessly into the context of this beautiful flower-filled garden.

My theme for this table setting is roses. We produce such a variety and I relish the chance to use so many of them together. The diversity of forms – from tight buds to blowsy garden roses – and huge colour range – from palest creamy yellow through deep mauve to rich red – means that using just one type of flower is in no way a restriction. The centrepiece for the main table is a glass footed bowl holding many summer garden roses

with some immature skimmia, showing green berries, as a contrast. The narrow base of the footed bowl is ideal for holding the stems in place and makes it easier to achieve a full, rounded look. Fresh strawberries placed on a china cake stand help to link all the colours together. Scattered randomly around the table are single roses and leaves and trailing ivy.

Standing near the table are repeated tall pedestals topped with wreaths of summer roses, in the centre of which stand glass cylinders containing a candle. The rose wreaths standing on the top of the pedestals are made using just one type of pink rose. The roses have been cut to the length required and then pushed into dry foam and are therefore very simple to make.

On the side table is an alabaster bowl holding many different coloured roses, some of which are still in bud. Rose leaves and trailing ivy have also been added. This arrangement actually contains about 50 different roses, in a myriad glowing colours. They are very tightly packed; this, together with the sheer number of roses used, helps create impact. If these were fresh flowers, obtaining such a variety would be tricky – they would need to be ordered especially – and very expensive. I can re-use this faux arrangement on table settings at other social occasions in and around my home.

ABOVE A pair of pedestals topped with wreaths of pink roses and grey foliage are positioned in front of the stone pillars. The wreaths can be reused as table centres or hung vertically as traditional door or wall wreaths. On the table trails of ivy are interspersed with individual rose heads ringed with foliage. In the central bouquet the mixed roses are combined with blossom and skimmia.

OPPOSITE On a side table, set with cups and saucers for serving tea after lunch, a lovely pure white footed alabaster bowl, packed with a huge variety of roses, echoes the centrepiece on the main table.

autumn flowers

autumn flower gallery

Orange, deep red, yellow and brown – these are the colours that represent the autumn season. Hydrangeas, which will be looking slightly dried by the autumn, are shown here in a deep red. The bright blue and pink colours of the natural flowers will start to fade into antiqued shades as autumn progresses, and some beautiful artificial 'dried' ones are shown on page 111. Hydrangeas are wonderful to use in flower arrangements throughout the year, but come spectacularly into their own in the autumn.

Dahlias are also wonderful – the range of colours is enormous, from white through to deepest red, as shown left. I grow many in my garden and they last until the first frost. Some of them reach immense heights and the heads are as large as dinner plates. They are not very good as a cut flower as they affect the water so badly and droop their heads within days. So, how wonderful to have our superb faux stems.

Autumn in the northern hemisphere is spring in the south, so we have included some varieties from countries such as Australia and South Africa in this collection, as their fresh counterparts, such as unusual orchids, arrive in our shops at this time.

hips and fruits
Apples, rose hips – such as these flaming orange ones – and berries predominate in the landscape in autumn, and faux versions are every bit as interesting as nature's bounty.

OPPOSITE, CLOCKWISE FROM TOP LEFT Dark burgundy elder berries clustered on a stem. The Chilean plant *Gaultheria mucronata* has berries that ripen to a lovely fuchsia colour and delicate green leaves. These luscious purple plums look like they are just about to drop from the tree. Hypericum berries – handpainted to represent the subtle shading on the berries – are enormously useful fillers in bouquets.

Autumn flowers have a beauty of their own. Faded roses and hydrangeas mark the progression from the huge array of shades available in the summer, while vibrant dahlias are a final defiant burst of colour against the backdrop of the changing leaves. These are indeed the 'days of mellow fruitfulness'.

OPPOSITE Gorgeous in summer and just as lovely in autumn, these faux dried hydrangea heads in a bronzed glass bowl are frozen in their glory. Fresh hydrangeas droop rapidly, as their woody stems do not take up water easily, but these last forever.

BELOW LEFT The subtle shades of this blue hydrangea and the pale pink roses in a glass bowl complement each other perfectly.

autumn flowers in the home

This lovely bronzed glass bowl is the perfect container for these fading hydrangea heads, right, that are shaded from pink to blue to soft brown – only the leaves retain their green colour. The texture of the petals, even down to the rustling sound they make when touched, means it is almost impossible to detect their artificiality. These are such useful faux flowers in autumn when fresh ones are not so abundant. This is shown to some effect in the picture on the left, where we have pushed the pale pink roses actually through the hydrangea head. These will be the last roses for this year. Some will be straggly and windblown but others, like these, will still be perfect.

I pick the last roses from my garden late into November. Living roses are, of course, available year round, so in any season they do not look out of place in your home. Some years ago, we dried millions (literally) of rose buds. My daughter and I were invited to a rose growers' convention in Nairobi. After the conference ended we were taken to five different locations to visit the growers. The scale was vast and I realized that, although we thought we were huge buyers, we were but minnows!

Approaching a faux flower arrangement is not very different from the way you would create a display of fresh flowers. When you are making a mixed bouquet, the starting point is to put together a good variety of material, including both flowers and foliage, that work well together in terms of shape, colour and form. The lovely glass bowl on the right is full of surprises. Fuchsia-coloured berries, elderberries, blackberries, skimmia, dahlias, clematis flowers in many colours and old English roses are all teamed together to produce a cacophony of colours – wonderful to cheer us on these shorter autumn days. This type of fresh material would be easy to pick from a well-stocked garden, but it can take a bit of time to build up a good stock of fake flowers until you have enough to mix and match in this way. Once you have such a collection, you can use and re-use your fakes in lots of ways.

Below, a glass bowl is filled with late plum branches – looking just as though they were gathered from the orchard as part of the final harvest. How right they look in this setting, with bright red apples sitting on the table. The stems supporting the weighty fruit must be anchored in place by use of acrylic water (for the technique see page 150).

ABOVE Autumn can have a final burst before colours start to fade, as this bowl of old English roses, clematis flowers, skimmia, black berries, pink berries and elderberries demonstrates.

LEFT Delicious looking but utterly false: a glass bowl filled with laden branches of purple plums.

In the glass vase above, we have used many differing shapes and colours of dahlias. One autumn I picked a large bunch of dahlias from my garden because frost (which is lethal for dahlias) had been forecast for the following night. Strangely, upon looking more closely at the bunch, I noticed that colours that should have clashed actually sat happily together. This, then, is a copy of that original selection; I love it and it has been admired greatly. I cannot tell you what immense pleasure it gives me to be able to recreate one-off displays in this way and to be able to capture and copy something so beautiful that nature has produced.

The other vase, more contemporary in shape, is very large and the dahlias are almost dinner plate size. Here the colours, although different from each other, link well because the burgundy stripe running through some of the white flowers tones with the deeper burgundy heads and the plain white flowers. This bouquet has been fixed in place with Stillwater™ resin to replicate water. Fortunately there are no earwigs inside these curling petals, as I have a horror of all creeping insects! So, no insects, and no dirty water – what an advantage in the busy lives we lead. When your faux flowers become dusty, we do have a special revitalizing spray available, but a damp cloth really does work wonders. A feather duster is helpful in between times.

ABOVE A delightful bowl of dahlias in all shades of pink, from full-blown flowers to tight buds. I used acrylic water to hold the stems just where I wanted them.

OPPOSITE This is a very elegant combination of dark burgundy, white and striped white and burgundy dahlias in a plain glass vase, and it works very well in a modern setting.

OPPOSITE An olive tree standard 'growing' in a ball of compost is set in a glass bowl. The glass gives it a very modern feel, but if you want a more traditional effect you can set the compost ball snugly into the top of a ceramic or terracotta pot.

RIGHT *Medinilla magnifica* in a ribbed terracotta vase that is as elegant as the flower it holds. Most faux flower stems are straight when you buy them, so remember to bend them into a more pleasing arching shape when you arrange them in a vase or they will never look natural.

After the glorious excesses of summer, it can be refreshing in the autumn to return to more minimal shapes and structures. This topiary olive tree, with its dark purple fruit, sits with its 'roots' shooting through the ball of compost, in a glass cylinder. Here it has been brought into the kitchen as if from the greenhouse. It would look stylish as a repeat design in the centre of a summer dining table, but do tell your guests not to eat the olives!

How popular this little tree has proved to be for city dwellers: no maintenance is needed, it attracts no insects and the olives do not fall from the tree. Real olive trees have proved increasingly popular in recent years even in countries with cooler, damper climates. It is true that, with a little extra care and attention in winter, potted specimens, especially, can be persuaded to survive away from their ideal Mediterranean

situation. However, live ones do not always look their best as the summer recedes, and yellowing leaves can spoil the overall effect, whereas faux ones always look in peak condition. This particular arrangement is very clean and modern in concept and would happily 'live' in a city apartment.

Medinilla magnifica is normally sold as a potted plant. Native to the Philippines, it is a majestic flowering plant with arching leaves and square woody stems that bear pink ball-shaped bracts, which open to reveal dangling clusters of flowers up to 50cm long. I first saw it at a friend's house; it had been growing for many years and had become enormous. This copy of a few flowering stems with some leaves and a bud is placed in an unusual ribbed terracotta container with a few contorted wooden twigs. The light from the window shows the flower to perfection.

OPPOSITE A table decorated ready
for a harvest supper with friends.
The abundant faux fruits and flowers
contribute to the relaxed informal
theme. The fake apples set into the
tall glass vases support the heavy
stems, as well as looking attractive,
and will not deteriorate as fresh
fruit very quickly does.

harvest supper

At this time of year when I have invited friends for a
relaxed meal it is nice to select a decorative theme based on the
seasonal theme of harvest offerings. Berries and fruits are the key
design "ingredients" for this supper table. This gives me a chance
to really showcase some remarkable artificial fruit.

    The two central arrangements are very large branches of
blackberries in glass vases, interspersed with leaves and roses.
The stems are held in place by hand-painted rosy apples, visible
inside the glass vases. The heavily fruited bramble branches, with
their distinctive soft green leaves, are allowed to sprawl in an
unstructured way, to resemble the way they grow in the wild.
Branches of drooping plums add to the feeling of plenty. The
roses are all coated in wax after they have been assembled.
The colours range from deepest burgundy to a pale lilac, and
echo the rich tones of the fruits.

    More trailing lengths of blackberry vines are laid on the
table itself, showing fruits in various stages of ripening, from green
to red to deepest black, just as they would be on a real bush.

I like to use fake fruit around my home all year round – the colours and shapes make wonderful decorations. A mixture of lots of different fruits placed together in plain glass or white ceramic bowls can look stunning. Or you can line up single varieties on a mantelpiece or window sill, such as a row of bright red apples. Apart from their longevity, they are indistinguishable from real fruit, which can occasionally cause a problem when peckish grandchildren come to call! But during the autumn months, to celebrate and reflect the incredible bounty that nature offers, they seem a particularly appropriate choice to combine with faux flowers.

Casually placed around the rest of the harvest table are larger pieces of fruit. This is a very casual display, and so easy to create, but the effect is remarkably beautiful. The different varieties I used include two types of pear, many sorts of apples, pomegranates, blackberries and plums.

LEFT The glowing orange colours of
fruit, berries and gourds set the scene
for a halloween table setting. A large
domed bunch of gerberas tops a
fishbowl filled with rosy apples.

halloween buffet

It is the end of October, the witches on their
broomsticks are abroad and the children are out trick or treating.
The supper is cooking awaiting their return, and the table is
laden with gourds, fruit, berries and flowers. What striking
colours this time of the year brings to our fading gardens. The
pumpkin is synonymous with halloween and the giant vegetables
and ornamental gourds are 'harvested' and ready to be carved
into weird faces and illuminated by candles. Taking a cue from
the pumpkin, the emphasis is certainly on orange.

The dark wooden pot holding berries is actually a burnt
wooden tree trunk – a most unusual container, it adds a tactile,
natural presence to this display. Next comes the giant pumpkin,
bulbous dried striped gourds of various types and sizes, a bright
yellow patty pan squash with fluted edges for a contrasting
highlight, and a deep red apple. Blackberries and cranberries, the
last cream rose and bright red rose hips complete the picture.

The only flowers in this setting apart from the cream rose
are the brilliant orange gerberas. A large glass bowl was filled with
faux apples into which I placed the stems of the gerberas and
some clematis foliage. This would be such an easy arrangement
for you to make at home for your own halloween buffet table.
No dry foam or setting agent is required as the flowers are held
in place by pushing the stems among the apples.

ABOVE What a sumptuous still life setting this is, the rich depths of colour in the pot pourri seed heads, dried berries and autumn fruits balanced beautifully by the sheen of the dark wood.

OPPOSITE A round fishbowl is filled with apples and stems of shaggy bright orange gerberas are pushed through the fruits, with trails of clematis vine tucked among them.

I love the picture these dried seed heads, berries and fruits make when carefully arranged in a still life so similar to those painted by the Old Masters. Here they stand against dark oak panelling, which helps to create this effect. The light coming from the window on the right hand side also adds to the ambience.

For our mail order catalogue 'Peony' we make many of these glass vases full of large seed heads and berries. After assembling them we pour a small amount of Stillwater™ resin over the seed heads to hold everything in place permanently. Similarly, the exotic berries, which resemble those of the hawthorn bush, are lightly set with resin to hold them in place within the confines of the burnt wooden vase.

winter flowers

OPPOSITE, CLOCKWISE FROM TOP LEFT Pure white snowdrops – the first of the year. Often seen in red, this white poinsettia flower, showing green buds and veining, is a refreshing alternative. These snowberries really stand out against their dark green leaves. A lovely hellebore flower shows the beautiful centres and stamens.

THIS PAGE With its velvety texture this brilliant red amaryllis flower is just sumptuous.

PREVIOUS PAGES A bowl of white amaryllis is echoed by another bowl of white phalaenopsis orchids.

winter flower gallery

Although they are thought of as spring flowers, snowdrops actually flower through the darkest days of winter, and how uplifting they are. Every year I start in January to look for the first flowers and this year I found the first clump of snowdrops half buried under dead leaves in the woods at home. Really, the time between the first frosts at the end of November and the joy of the first snowdrops is only a couple of months. Afterwards we have hellebores, or Christmas roses – a friend of mine holds the National Collection and his garden is a delight to visit in winter. The faux hellebore shown opposite is a particularly lovely.

The white poinsettia, which in Britain cannot survive our frosty weather, makes a wonderful flowering houseplant at this time of the year. A deep pink poinsettia plant can be seen on page 136. Flowering amaryllis bulbs are also popular in our homes during and just after the Christmas season. The close-up shot left shows how carefully each petal has been shaped, shaded and constructed to make this impressive and very popular flower. The berries on real snowberry plants are poisonous to humans, so the fake ones are less of a concern.

orchids Orchids are possibly the very best artificial flower available, and even I need to touch them to be certain that they were either grown or made. We have them in an amazing array of colours, but white is always the very best seller. The flower head shown here is of a superb cattleya orchid. From the shaping of the outer sepals to the hand painting of the lip which contains the stamens it is a work of art.

OPPOSITE, CLOCKWISE FROM TOP LEFT Bright orange slipper orchids with their glossy modified lips, which give them their name. Cream and burgundy vanda orchids. Bright orange disa orchids. Pale pink cymbidium orchids.

At this time of year, when the days are short and we seldom see the sun, the need for flowers to cheer the dark winter days becomes ever more important. Brilliant reds and shades of white become the order of the day, and the exotic plants, flowers and orchids from the southern hemisphere are now in season, adding even more colours to our palette.

winter flowers in the home

The winter season in our factory at Ruckley is very busy and our home seems to be permanently full of guests, so I have no time to spend hours arranging flowers. But entertaining, whether casually in the kitchen or more formally in the dining room, requires flowers, so I rely heavily on fakes.

The bright red amaryllis on the opposite page are hand tied and set into a glass cylinder. To make this large arrangement you will need round dry foam to which the amaryllis stems are glued and then tied with red cord. It is initially expensive to make, but can be brought out year after year. A less expensive method of manufacture would be to glue tall leaves to the dry foam and then push two or three stems of amaryllis into the centre. Fresh amaryllis stems can also be very expensive, and they last such a short time.

The large amaryllis wreath on the left was very simply made using dry foam as a base, cutting the amaryllis heads to the length and inserting them into the foam. If you are using a cane or willow base, then you can either wire or glue the heads in place. The berries are used to reflect and highlight the flowers. One year I so loved the wreath I made for my front door that I left it hanging in situ well into the spring. Imagine my astonishment to find a robin nesting in it. She reared her young that spring and returned the following three years, rearing her families on our front door. Like me she obviously did not mind that the flowers and foliage were artificial. Sadly one winter she came and slept in the wreath for two nights, but we found her dead on the doorstep after the third night. Many tears were shed.

LEFT This huge fluted glass vase is just packed with protea flowers and large pointed aloe leaves. I like the fact that the stems and leaves are visible through the clear glass. A small wooden bowl holds a single protea stem, cut short.

BELOW Four black ostrich eggs are filled with faux feathers and grasses. The eggs are glued together in a group of four, making a very dramatic statement against the pale yellow background. These could well be used as a table setting. I used white ostrich eggs to decorate an Easter breakfast table (see pages 78 to 81), and it is amazing what a different effect painting them black makes.

ABOVE The richness of this vibrant pink velvet poinsettia is matched by the gleaming black metal disc container in which it is 'growing'.

BELOW A rose set in a pretty glass vase. Flowers such as roses, freesias, ranunculus, orchids, even tulips, seem to be on offer year round, so having their faux counterparts on display in your homes seems sensible to me.

The proteas shown on the previous page are grown mostly in the southern hemisphere, including both Australia and South Africa – their summer being our winter. This is why I have shown them in this, our winter section. The arrangement was originally made for a friend's birthday party. She lives partly in Cape Town and wanted a flower native to this region. The glass vase is fluted and very large, and to add interest we added pointed aloe leaves. For emphasis we placed a single stem into a wooden African bowl.

The bracts of the poinsettia shown above are a vibrant pink, which is an unusual colour but looks wonderfully warm and bright. It is set in a metal container, and we have covered the dry foam with black polished stones to complement the black bowl. Low displays are very useful around the home, and this one would look equally charming against a lighter background.

The glass vase in which this bright orange-red rose is sitting is ideal for displaying a single flower. Flower heads always look their best when set off by some foliage, even if it is just a few leaves – they can look a little lost otherwise. For advice on how to cut fake flowers to get the most material from a single stem see page 156.

On the opposite page is a repeat design using snowdrops, the flower that sees us through the final days of winter. Grouped together, they are so endearing in the pretty glasses in which they are set. We have left the bulbs and roots visible so that the snowdrops look as if they are still growing.

These snowdrops are lovely massed in the centre of a winter table, and would be a perfect choice for a winter wedding.

Fake flowers can be sited almost everywhere that fresh flowers can be used, the main difference being the length of time that the fake flowers can stay in situ. The other advantage is their amenability to being shaped or pushed into any design or container. Orchids, for example, can be twisted and manipulated to accommodate the container in which they are to be displayed.

White cymbidium orchids make a spectacular winter display. Cymbidium plants are usually available to buy at this time of the year. Here I set our fake one into a very large black metal container. The dry foam is covered in black polished stones, through which the roots are visible, adding to the realism of the arrangement. Each stem has also been tied to a bamboo stake with wired raffia to enhance the impression of a living plant. This is such a large display, it would be ideal for an entrance hall to welcome guests, but it would make an equally strong statement in any room.

To the right, standing in a lovely Victorian conservatory, we have placed a large terracotta pot containing mauve vanda orchids. The pot has been aged by adding a light covering of moss – you could simply use a pot that has been standing in your garden over winter and achieved the same effect naturally over time. The whole arrangement stands about 135cm high. The plant is set into dry foam covered with 'soil' made from dyed sawdust, but the foam could as easily be covered with large polished stones. If you are assembling this type of arrangement yourself at home, where the weight will not cause problems for transportation, you could simply fill your pot with dry compost and plunge your fake stems straight into it. Do not water the soil though. The beauty of the leaves certainly helps to add to the total realism of these orchids. The mauve, hand painted flowers bring life and colour to this unheated conservatory and the plant itself does not mind the winter temperatures.

ABOVE These tall purple vanda orchids in a terracotta pot are completely unfussed by plunging night time temperatures in this light and airy conservatory.

OPPOSITE This large potted white cymbidium plant is fake – hard to tell, particularly if you use real bamboo to support the flower stems.

christmas

This is the most opulent time of the year; when excesses are allowed and indeed encouraged. Families gather and friends visit so our homes need to look extra beautiful and welcoming. Ironically, though, we are at our busiest, and time to devote to decoration is at a premium, especially on the day itself. How wonderful then, to be able to plan your dinner table flowers in advance, and have them all prepared and ready to go so that all you need do is place them on the table.

The setting of the Christmas dinner table is of utmost importance: it is the central point of the whole celebration. For the large table arrangement I used a huge flared glass vase and half filled it with deep red amaryllis petals. This was topped with a large hand-tied bunch of red-berried holly, and some apples on stems. I placed wreaths around the very tall silver and crystal candelabras made of red roses, skimmia and rose leaves. Another wreath, using red velvet amaryllis, pomegranates, apples and holly sits on a sideboard, and I also made matching swags to hang either on the mantelpiece or a staircase, echoing the theme throughout the house. In the central white urn sit faux fruit nestled in ivy foliage. The individual small arrangements shown on the left, on the sideboard and on the table itself, are again made using red amaryllis. What a traditional Christmas this is.

OPPOSITE Silver and crystal candelabras set an elegant tone, supplemented by sumptuous red flowers and fruits. A combination of heights in the flower arrangements makes a more interesting looking table and allows for the free flow of conversation between your guests.

LEFT, ABOVE AND BELOW The small arrangements on the main table and on a sideboard feature amaryllis flowers cut short and placed in gold etched glasses. A wreath studded with holly, pomegranates and more amaryllis heads is propped up behind, and bright silver Christmas tree baubles provide the finishing touch.

RIGHT An all-white theme is becoming increasingly popular for Christmas table decorations, especially among those people looking for a a style that will not jar with a modern interior.

LEFT As an alternative to the traditional red of holly berries, why not use fruiting ivy or white-berried faux plants, such as these snowberries?

Here we see a more modern – but nonetheless stunning – interpretation of the Christmas table. Huge amaryllis, ivy, snowdrops, giant fir cones, baubles and berries have all been used, all conforming to the white and green theme. On either side of the table hand-tied amaryllis stems were been placed in glass spheres and set with black stones and ivy. In the centre is a very long metal container in which bulbs of white amaryllis are 'growing', complete with their buds and leaves, interspersed with white snowdrops and ivy. Large dried seed heads and moss have been used to cover the dry foam.

This setting could also be used as the centrepiece for a large buffet table, perhaps on New Year's Eve. It is of a more modern genre and would be fitting in a minimalist home.

Many other designs shown throughout the book could also be used at this time of year, as centrepieces on your table or around the home – such as the camellias shown on page 17, the white amaryllis on page 32, the snowdrops on page 34, the bright pink amaryllis on page 42 and the basket of hyacinths on page 50. As all of these flowers are artificial, the Christmas preparations can be spread over a far longer period, preventing the last-minute panic when there is so much to be done, and allowing you time to enjoy creating your floral decorations.

valentine supper

Red roses mean, of course, 'I love you', so what other flower could be used on this table setting, on this special evening? The scene must be romantic, the table set for two, with candles, flowers and background music to complete the scene.

On the right of the table lies a hand-tied bouquet of red roses ready to be presented to a lady from her lover. The vases used are all small crystal perfume bottles in a very modern design, which suit the romantic mood perfectly. The roses are all different – though all red – and placed at varying heights. How wonderful that all these flowers can be kept and treasured as a reminder of this romantic supper. On a more prosaic note, I can never believe how incredibly expensive red roses are on Valentine's day. But producing so many identical real flowers of consistent quality at the same time must be a logistical nightmare for the rose growers, and this is their prime selling period. Faux roses remain the same price throughout the year, and retain their beauty always.

LEFT Undeniably elegant and romantic, this Valentine table is also understated and classical. Too fussy or feminine a theme can be offputting if you are trying to woo a man!

RIGHT To enhance the romantic mood, continue the theme around the rest of the room, setting roses on side tables, windowsills and mantelpieces.

LEFT The hand-tied bouquet of red roses is studded with foliage and tied with a silver silk ribbon. It can of course be kept forever as a memento of a truly special evening.

OPPOSITE A close-up showing the stoppers from the perfume bottles placed around the table. The spiky foliage of skimmia seeds adds a contrasting touch.

BELOW A single red rose placed in a modern square crystal perfume bottle.

The selection of crystal perfume bottles used on the table setting are both decorative in their own right – their many facets helping to reflect light from the candle – and also act as miniature vases for single roses. The bottles are of a modern, square-cut design and are complete with their stoppers, some of which are casually placed on the table to add further interest. None of the roses has been set permanently into the perfume bottles with acrylic water, so that all of these can be recycled for another occasion in a different style of vase, or you could include them in mixed short-stem bowl arrangements, such as those shown on page 15 or page 21.

The pretty bouquet shown above contains red velvet rose buds, more open flowers and spiky burgundy rose hips. It is simple to make – see page 157 for instructions for hand-tied bouquets. The fact that all the roses are different and show varying colours really does make them more interesting. I find using uniform flowers in any arrangement creates an artificial look, as in life, all flowers are different.

working with fake flowers

1   2   3

setting flowers in resin

While writing about the arrangements in this book, I have tried to explain how some of them are made. This section relates to specific fixing agents that you can use at home. In our factory Stillwater™ resin is used extensively but I do realize that not everyone will have access to this amazing artificial 'water' when working with faux flowers. We use resin on a daily basis, as our arrangements are shipped everywhere, and would be unstable if not firmly fixed into their containers. The clarity of the resin has to be perfect as it replicates pure spring water. After making the arrangements we place them carefully onto racks in our heated drying houses, where they cure for about three days.

Prior to drying it is imperative that the arrangements are not moved otherwise a rippled effect will occur in the resin. It is also important not to allow resin to drip onto the side of the vase as it will remain there forever. Protective gloves must be worn at all times. It is vital that none of the resin is spilt on any surface. We do however, sell the resin and, if used with great care, it can be a very successful product. Simpler methods of fixing are described on the following pages.

How to set flowers in resin

Before mixing the resin it is imperative that you have cut the flowers to suit your design.

1   Full instructions are given on the packet. But as a guide, pour one bottle of resin into a disposable plastic container.

2   Add the second bottle of fixing agent. With a disposable spatula stir the chemicals together, taking care not to spill even a spot.

3   Carefully pour the mixture into the vase, but do not let the resin touch the sides of the vase. Insert the flowers into the vase, ensuring that all stems are pushed right into the resin. Leave to dry for at least three days in a warm place.

Make sure you only mix enough resin for the vase you wish to fill. Any excess must be disposed of carefully. It must never be poured down a household sink or drain. Throw away the mixing receptacle and the spatula used to mix the two chemicals.

White gerberas and freesias set in clear resin. This flower fixing method is slightly tricky, but the finished result does look remarkably like water.

arranging without water

If you do not have access to our wonderful resin, here are some different methods of fixing artificial flowers into their containers. The first uses twisted white stems, and on the opposite page we have used polished stones. Plastic ice chips, marbles, moss, nuts and seed heads can all be used successfully. Sometimes, if I am using a treasured vase at home I place marbles, stones or plastic ice chips into the base and simply add tap water. However the stems and the vase will need washing after a few weeks if the tap water discolours. Plastic-coated stems will not discolour the water, but a cut stem where the central wire is revealed will show signs of rust after a time.

1

Using twisted twigs

1 Line a straight sided glass bowl with coils of pliable twisted willow. This is available in a range of natural shades as well as white.

2 Cut the stems of the flowers you are using and push them down through the willow, which will hold them in place. I used David Austin™ roses and leaves, mixed with green *Viburnum opulus*.

2

1

Using pebbles and leaves

1 Firstly line your bowl with large green fleshy leaves. Then fill it almost to the top with polished stones.

2 Insert the flower stems, the leaves and the roots through the stones. Add more stones on top to anchor tall stems, such as the green cymbidium orchids shown.

2

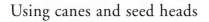

Using canes and seed heads

1 Tie tall floppy stems, such as those of phalaenopsis orchids, to a cane using wired raffia. Cord, garden twine or plain raffia would be acceptable alternatives.

2 These are giant walnuts, but any heavy seed heads, cones, or stones could be used instead to anchor the stems.

3 This shows the finished arrangement. The orchid and leaves have been inserted into the centre of the nuts.

1

2

3

ringing the changes

This glass ring is ideal for showing a variety
of flowers. I selected it as the flowers can be changed
seasonally as they do not need to be 'set', but are simply
cut to size. The leaves are tied to the individual flowers
using wired raffia. Although I have used glass vases that
are physically linked, using a dozen or so small flower
vases would give the same effect.

Making a seasonal arrangement

1 Create individual posies of foliage or flowers
by binding the stems with decorative twine.

2 When each vase is filled you can place a
candle in the centre.

3 For a different effect, use a completely
different selection of flowers.

1

2

3

Cutting a single stem

1 It is very important to ensure that each cut is directly above a leaf, so that when the entire stem is inserted into the vase none of the cuts is visible.

2 All of the parts, including the lower leaves, can be used.

1

2

maximizing single stems

All day we cut flowers in our Shropshire factory. The first thing we teach our staff is that no cuts must be visible in the finished arrangement. If a part of the plastic stem with the wire centre is visible then the whole natural look is ruined. In the picture on the right all that you can see is the rose, one stem and the leaves. No cuts are visible. This is much easier to achieve if ceramic vases are used instead of glass. If you use a glass vase, then hand tie the rose and the leaves so that the cuts in the stem are hidden under raffia or ribbon.

RIGHT This is the way we made
the bouquet of ranunculus featured
on page 72. The length of the
stems was shortened to fit into
the bowl, and the flowers are held
in place using twisted willow.

1

hand-tied arrangements

Making a hand-tied posy

1 In your left hand place the first
stem to be used, so that the head
rests between the thumb and
forefinger. Continue until all flowers
and leaves have been used. Slightly
twist the stems and tie with wired
raffia. A ribbon can be added at this
point. It sounds easy, but it takes a
little practice to make them perfect.

2 When the bunch is finished and
tightly tied, trim the stems to one
length. Always test the length of
the stems against the vase you are
hoping to use. It is so annoying
to cut the stems and then find
that they are too short!

2

We now make a large selection of hand-tied flowers
because of their ever-increasing popularity. They can be placed
directly into any container without the need for further arranging,
so are a useful gift. We make many of them for inclusion in our
bridal range, both for the bride and bridesmaids. They are also
useful gifts for the bride's mother and mother-in-law and can be
given to them during the speeches at the wedding reception. This
memento can be kept as a permanent reminder of a happy day.
Fresh flowers, although an equally wonderful gift, will normally
have died before the happy couple return from their honeymoon.

The flowers easiest to use and best suited for hand-tied
bouquets are roses, sweetpeas, ranunculus, clematis heads (as
shown in the steps left), anemones, cala lilies, freesias and
dahlias. Mixed flowers can also look wonderful.

suppliers

UK

Peony Direct
www.peonydirect.com
(Still Water™ resin/hardener kits available)

Ruckley
www.ruckley.com
(Still Water™ resin/hardener kits available)

Blue Diamond Garden Group
www.bluediamond.gg/gardencentres.htm
01481 231100

Burford Garden Centres
www.burford.co.uk
01993 823117

Dobbies Garden Centres
www.dobbies.co.uk
0131 663 6778

Frosts Group
www.frostsgroup.com
01908 583511

Garden & Leisure Group
www.g-l.co.uk

Haskins Garden Centres Limited
www.haskins.co.uk
02380 472324

John Lewis
www.johnlewis.com
08456 049 049

Klondyke Garden Centres
www.klondykegardencentres.co.uk
01324 712263

Lakeland Limited
www.lakeland.co.uk
01539 488200

Museum Selection
www.museumselection.co.uk
01993 851166

Next
ww.next.co.uk
0844 8448939

RHS Enterprises Limited
www.rhs.org.uk
01483 212396

Webbs of Wychbold
www.webbsofwychbold.co.uk
01527 861555

Westgate Department Stores
www.arcs.co.uk
01733 887930

Wyevale Garden Centres
www.wayvale.co.uk
0844 800 8428

USA

Bloomingdales
www.bloomingdales.com
1 866 593 2540

Crate & Barrel
www.crateandbarrel.com
1 800 967 6696

Michaels Stores
www.michaels.com
1 800 642 4235

Neiman Marcus
www.neimannmarcus.com
1 800 888 4757

Pottery Barn
www.potterybarn.com
1 888 779 5176

Restoration Hardware
www.restorationhardware.com
1 800 910 9836

Target Home Stores
www.target.com
1 800 440 0680

Suppliers of acrylic water kits:

Afloral.com
www.afloral.com
1 888 299 4100

Amazon Foliages
www.amazonfoliages.com
1 866 606 1167

Kinkade Studios
www.kinkadestudios.com
1 866 606 1167

Floral Supply.com
www.floralsupply.com
1 800 827 7366

author's acknowledgements

First of all, thanks to my friend Jennifer Walton, for her help and encouragement.

To my friends Robert and Gill Burton for the loan of their house.

Our Dutch designers – Jerome Letens and Paul-Pierre Leysen – both of whom are wonderful friends and inspirational.

My husband, Keith Ashbourne, for all his support, emotional and financial!

My two daughters, sons-in-law and four delightful grandchildren, who all love flowers as much as I do.

For my so patient staff, Richard Brewin, Paul Atkins, Denise Preece, Sherri Nash, Gareth Shell and all the girls who work so diligently day after day.

Debbie Poulter and Sheila Jones, Jackie Dawes and Sue McGraw for feeding and housing all the constant visitors to Ruckley, and, of course, Pat Roberts, who grows all the flowers at Ruckley.

Jacqui Small, publisher, for inviting me to write the book, Sian Parkhouse, editor, Maggie Town, art director, Sian Irvine, photographer, her assistant Joe Giacomet, and Emma Cassi, stylist.

All the wonderful Chinese flower producers who constantly amaze me with the beauty and accuracy of the flowers they make for us, Dick Chiu, our agent, and Gert Bulk for all his dried flowers.

Also all my English friends, whose passion for gardens and gardening equals my own, Sally, Penny, Sue and Jen.